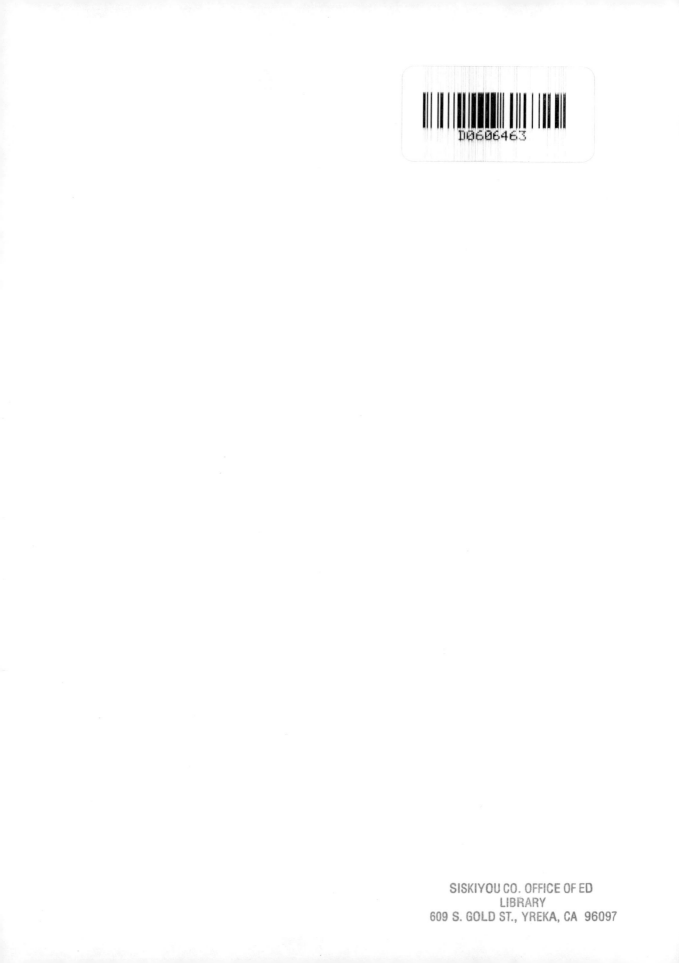

The Rourke Guide to State Symbols

STATE SEALS

David and Patricia Armentrout

Rourke Publishing LLC
Vero Beach, Florida 32964

www.rourkepublishing.com

PHOTO CREDITS:
Visual Information Support Center, United States National Guard, Nashville,
Tennessee

COVER ILLUSTRATION: Jim Spence

EDITORIAL SERVICES:
Pamela Schroeder

Library of Congress Cataloging-in-Publication Data

Armentrout, David and Patricia
    State seals / David and Patricia Armentrout
      p. cm. — (The Rourke guide to state symbols)
    Includes index
    ISBN 1-58952-087-4
    1. Seals (Numismatics)—United States—States—Juvenile literature. 2. United
States—Juvenile literature. I. Armentrout, Patricia, 1960- II. Title. III. Series.

    CD5603 .A76 2001   2001034910
    737.6.0973—dc21

Printed in the USA

TABLE OF CONTENTS

INTRODUCTION

A seal is a design. In ancient times, a seal was a carved design used to mark objects or papers. Seal designs were carved into wood, metal, stone, and gemstones.

Some seal designs were carved into rings. A seal ring was worn by an important person like a king. The king's important papers were sealed with hot wax. The ring was pressed into the wax and the carved design appeared. The king's papers were marked and sealed with his own special design.

A state seal is a special design, too. Every state has a seal that is a symbol of statehood. The seal appears on all important state documents. A seal design can also appear on wall plaques in government buildings. For instance, a state seal is often seen behind a judge's bench in a courtroom.

Many of the state seal designs change over the years. The designs in this book best represent the seal chosen by each state. Each seal stands for the state's pride and history.

ALABAMA

Senate and House members make laws for their states. The Alabama seal was chosen by the Alabama Senate and House in 1939. The design in use today is also the first design used in 1819, the year Alabama became a state. However, in 1869, lawmakers approved a new seal. It was used until 1939, when the original seal was reapproved. The seal design shows the outline of the state with its major rivers.

ALASKA

Alaska's seal shows a mix of natural wildlife and Alaska's growth in industry. The seal is a circle 2 1/8 inches (5.4 cm) in diameter. Inside are mountains and icebergs. Northern lights shine above. Fish and marine seals represent Alaska wildlife. Sailing ships, a farming scene,  and a railroad show Alaska's growth in industry. Around the center design are the words "The Seal of the State of Alaska."

ARIZONA

1912, printed on the bottom of this seal, is the year Arizona became a state. In the center are mountains and a sunrise. They stand for the natural beauty and sunny climate of the state. A miner holds a pick axe and shovel. Arizona has a history of mining. Old mining towns are now a  tourist attraction in Arizona. Copper mining is a big industry today.

Arkansas' seal design shows an eagle with a scroll in its beak. The eagle holds an olive branch in one claw and a bundle of arrows in the other. A shield covers the front of the eagle. Inside the shield are three pictures. The top picture is of a steamboat. Steamboats were a form of transportation on the state's rivers. The other pictures represent farming. They show a plow, a beehive, and a sheaf of wheat.

California's seal was designed by a member of the U.S. Army. It was adopted in 1849. California became a state in 1850. The seal has 31 stars on its upper edge. The stars stand for the 31 states that were trying to enter the Union at the time California was. The mountains and water display California's natural beauty. "Eureka" means "I Found It" and describes the miner digging for gold.

Colorado shows its year of statehood, 1876, at the bottom of its seal. The seal was approved in 1877 by the Colorado General Assembly. The design changed very little from the Colorado Territory seal.

The pick axe and sledge hammer pictured at the bottom are miner's tools. The snowcapped mountains at the top of the shield stand for Colorado's majestic Rocky Mountains.

CONNECTICUT

The first seal of Connecticut was brought over from England in 1639. It was used by the Connecticut Colony until 1687. Colony control changed and the seal disappeared. A different seal had to be used.

A new seal was designed in 1711. It was larger and more oval in shape. After the Revolutionary War the seal changed from a colony seal to a state seal. Statehood was granted in 1788.

Delaware was the first state. Statehood was granted December 7, 1787. The farmer with his hoe shows the importance of farming. On the right, the militiaman with his musket represents the people who fought for the rights of all who live there.

There are three dates listed on the bottom. In 1793 the farmer and militiaman were removed from the seal. In 1847 they were put back into the design. In 1907 the seal was updated again to show "Great Seal of The State of Delaware."

Florida's first state seal was designed in 1868. It showed the sun's rays, a steamboat on water, a female Indian scattering flowers, and a cocoa tree. In 1970 the cocoa tree was replaced with the sabal palmetto tree.

Other changes were made to the Florida seal. The Indian's headdress was removed to make her look more like a Seminole Indian. A mountain in the background was eventually flattened.

The Great Seal of Georgia honors the Constitution. The seal was adopted by the state in 1798. Statehood was granted in 1788.

"Wisdom, Justice, and Moderation" is Georgia's motto. The motto is displayed on three pillars that support an arch. 1776 represents the Declaration of Independence.

The Georgia seal has a reverse side design that shows a farmer plowing a field. The reverse seal reads "Agriculture and Commerce 1776."

"State of Hawaii 1959" is displayed on the top of Hawaii's state seal. Hawaii gained statehood in 1959. The bottom quote translates to "The life of the land is perpetuated in righteousness." The quote is believed to have come from Hawaii's King Kamehameha III.

The inside picture shows King Kamehameha I, on the left, holding a staff. On the right is the female figure Liberty with the Hawaiian flag.

IDAHO

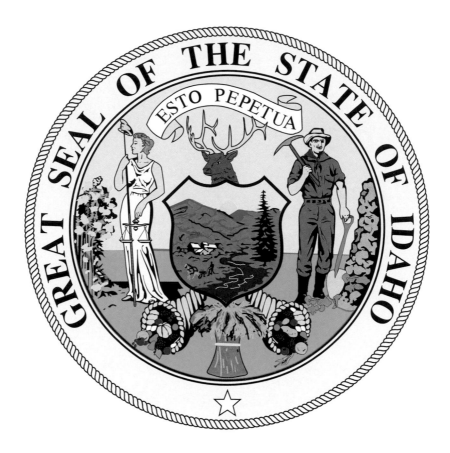

Idaho became a state in 1890. The seal was designed by Emma Edwards Green. She entered a contest with other artists. Green won $100 for her design.

Emma Green's design has a horn of plenty, or cornucopia, to represent farming. The river is the Snake River. A miner stands for Idaho's industry. The woman in white stands for justice. Green used the female figure because she believed Idaho women would soon win the right to vote.

ILLINOIS

Illinois gained statehood in 1818. That year appears just below 1868, the year the current seal was adopted. August 26, 1818, is the date of the state's first constitution.

The eagle holds a shield in its talons. The 13 stars and 13 stripes on the shield stand for the original 13 states, or colonies.

INDIANA

This official state seal of Indiana was adopted in 1963. Similar seals were used in Indiana as early as 1801.

The Indiana seal design uses leaves of the tulip tree, the state tree, to decorate its outer ring. The year 1816 is the year Indiana became a state. A woodsman, a buffalo, sycamore trees, hills, and a setting sun make up the center of the seal design.

IOWA

The Iowa seal was chosen in 1847, 1 year after Iowa became a state. The state motto is written on a scroll in the eagle's mouth. The eagle and scroll also appear on the Iowa state flag.

A soldier holding an American flag stands center stage in the seal. Surrounding the soldier are symbols of Iowa's history, including a wheat field a cabin and a ship on a river.

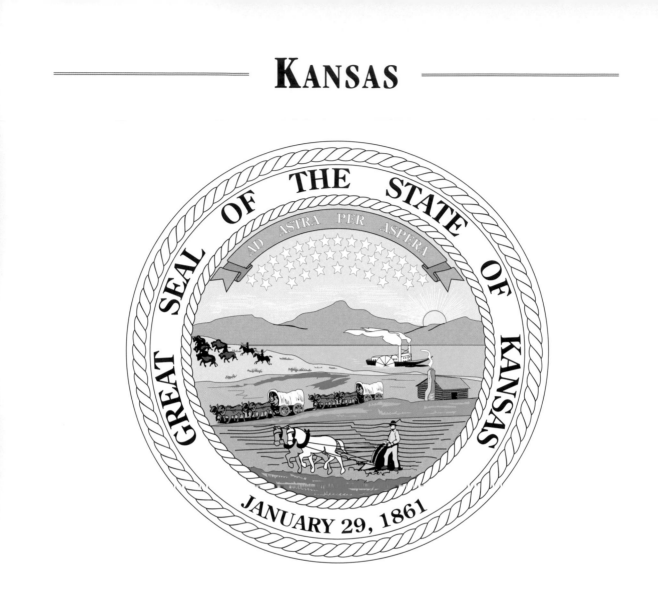

White stars show up well against the blue background in the Kansas seal. The state motto above the stars means "To the stars through difficulties."

The steamboat on the river stands for commerce, or trade. The man plowing stands for agriculture, or farming. Historic wagons go west across the green plains, and Indians on horseback hunt buffalo. Kansas became the 34th state January 29, 1861.

KENTUCKY

Kentucky has used this simple seal design since 1792. However, some changes were made over the years. The seal now shows two men, one in formal dress and the other in buckskin. They are in a friendly embrace. Earlier seals have shown both men wearing buckskin, both men wearing formal clothes, and the men shaking hands. The phrase "United We Stand, Divided We Fall" is the Kentucky state motto.

LOUISIANA

The Louisiana seal is different than most state seals. It highlights the state bird, the pelican. Louisiana is also nicknamed the "Pelican State."

At one time the seal showed a mother pelican feeding a dozen chicks in her nest. Pelicans do not normally have that many chicks at one time, so the design was changed to show a more realistic number.

The state seal of Maine was designed just months after Maine became a state. Many changes have been made since 1820.

The present design was made in 1919. It shows the North Star with "Dirigo" written below it. Dirigo means "I Direct."

Maine is covered with about 90 percent forests and trees. The pine tree, the water, the woodsman, and the moose represent Maine's natural beauty. The seaman represents Maine as a coastal state.

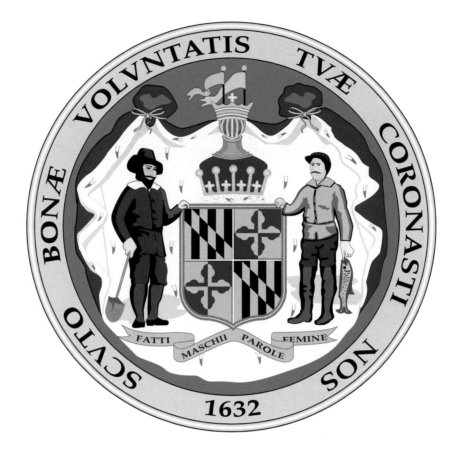

Maryland became the 7th state in 1788. This Maryland seal was chosen in 1876. It is the reverse design of the seal. The obverse, or front, design shows Lord Baltimore, a knight, on a horse.

This reverse design is the side most often seen. A farmer and a fisherman support a shield. The words on the banner beneath them translates to "Strong deeds, gentle words."

The Massachusetts seal was chosen by Governor John Hancock in 1780. Hancock was also the first person to sign the Declaration of Independence.

The Indian holds an arrow pointing down, showing he is a peaceful man. The star represents Massachusetts as one of the original 13 states. The Latin words in the ribbon describe the arm and sword above the shield. The words mean, "By the sword we seek peace, but peace only under liberty."

MICHIGAN

Michigan is made up of two peninsulas. A peninsula is a section of land surrounded by water on three sides. The words below the shield on the Michigan seal mean, "If you seek a pleasant peninsula, look about you." The Michigan seal boasts its natural beauty, which was formed by the Great Lakes. An elk, moose, and eagle represent Michigan wildlife.

MINNESOTA

The Minnesota seal shows a farmer planting his field along the Mississippi River. An Indian is on horseback in the background. The seal proudly displays the year Minnesota became a state—1858. The state motto "L'Etoile du Nord" means "Star of the North."

This seal design is on the state flag. Another design has the words "The Great Seal of the State of Minnesota" around the center picture.

MISSISSIPPI

Mississippi gained statehood in 1817. It was the 20th state. The seal has the same design that was used while Mississippi was still a territory. The seal has been in use since 1798.

The Mississippi seal is very patriotic. It displays our national symbol, the American eagle. The eagle holds its head up high as it clutches an olive branch in one claw and a quiver of arrows in the other.

MISSOURI

Missouri became the 24th state in 1820. The small stars represent the states in the Union at that time. The large star represents Missouri. Two giant grizzly bears support the center shield. The crescent moon in the shield stands for the newness and potential growth of the state. The bear below the moon stands for strength and bravery. The bald eagle is a national symbol.

The seal of the Montana Territory was changed before it became the seal for the state. Montana is represented by the mountains on the left and the falls of the Missouri River on the right.

The seal also shows a farmer's plow and a miner's pick axe and shovel. These items symbolize Montana's fertile land and mineral wealth.

Nebraska's first official state seal was made the same year Nebraska became a state—1867. A steamboat on the Missouri River and a train in the background show historic transportation in Nebraska. In the foreground, or front of the seal, is a blacksmith working. Sheaves of wheat show Nebraska as a farming state.

NEVADA

President Lincoln proclaimed Nevada a state in 1864. In 1866 the state motto "All for Our Country" was added to the seal design.

Nevada is rich in mineral resources. The seal has a silver miner loading ore into a cart at the opening of a mountain. A quartz mill stands in front of another mountain. Farming is represented by a sheaf of wheat, a sickle, and a plow.

NEW HAMPSIIIRE

The New Hampshire seal went through a period of change. At one time it showed a pine tree and a fish. They stood for the state's resources. The seal changed to show a ship on stocks to represent Portsmouth as the state's ship-building center. The seal now shows the frigate *Raleigh*. It was one of the Navy's first ships.

NEW JERSEY

The New Jersey seal was chosen in 1777. Although the U.S. officially gained independence in 1776, small battles still occurred with the British. For this reason, seal designers met at a tavern to discuss the design. It was at the tavern where the official design was accepted. The horse's head in the seal stands for strength. The two female figures stand for Liberty and Prosperity.

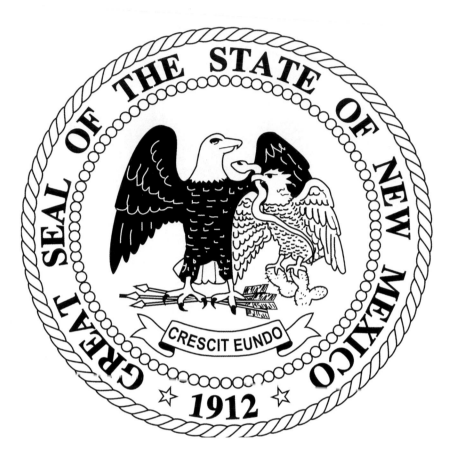

The seal of New Mexico shows a large American eagle stretching its wings out over a smaller Mexican eagle. The motto in the banner means "It grows as it goes." The seal image was used when New Mexico was just a territory. When New Mexico became a state in 1912, the words "Great Seal of the State of New Mexico" and the statehood date were added to the design.

The New York state seal is also the state's official coat of arms. A coat of arms is a combination of symbols and pictures. The symbols and pictures describe the history, or heritage, of a place or a person.

Notice the American eagle standing on the globe. The globe shows the part of the North Atlantic Ocean where New York is located.

North Carolina

In 1971 the General Assembly of North Carolina decided to make a standard state seal design. Before then, the seal design kept changing. Today the design shows "Liberty" on the left and "Plenty" on the right. "Plenty" displays a big horn of plenty, or cornucopia. "Liberty" holds a pole with a cap. A three-masted ship sails the waters in the background.

North Dakota

The North Dakota seal shows a single tree in the middle of a prairie. This image is a symbol of how big and open North Dakota is. It is a state with very few large cities.

The seal also shows an Indian on horseback. North Dakota is proud of its Indian heritage. North Dakota is nicknamed the "Sioux State."

The Ohio seal has changed many times. A modern seal was designed in 1967. It was changed in 1996. A design from 1847 can be seen in the state house in Columbus. That design is hand-painted on a skylight. Over the years, the slightly different designs have all shown a bundle of arrows, a sheaf of wheat, and a sun rising over mountains.

Oklahoma was made the 46th state in 1907. The large star in the center of this seal stands for Oklahoma. Oklahoma honors five Indian Nations in the points of the star—the Chickasaw, Choctaw, Seminole, Creek, and Cherokee tribes. An Indian shaking hands with a white man stands for the merging cultures.

OREGON

The Oregon seal has 33 stars showing it was the 33rd state. Two ships sail in the background. One British ship sails away from shore. It stands for the end of British power. The second ship is an American ship coming towards shore. It stands for American independence.

Symbols of early settlement and farming are represented by the covered wagon, the plow, and a sheaf of wheat.

The design of the Pennsylvania seal includes a crest, or shield. Three symbols are on the shield. The ship under full sail stands for commerce, or trade. The plow stands for labor and strong will. The sheaves of wheat represent farming in Pennsylvania. A stalk of corn and an olive branch surround the shield. The eagle on top symbolizes power.

RHODE ISLAND

    Rhode Island is the smallest state. It consists of a mainland and 36 islands. The words "Providence Plantations" in the outer ring honor the early settlements on the largest island. That island has the same name as the state.

    Rhode Island has used an anchor as one of its symbols for hundreds of years. Rhode Island added the state motto "Hope" above the anchor in 1644.

SOUTH CAROLINA

The seal design of South Carolina represents a Revolutionary War battle. Inside the left oval stands a palm tree. It represents victory. A fallen tree stands for the defeat of the British fleet. The woman in the right oval stands for hope. The ovals are connected by branches of the state tree—the palmetto.

SOUTH DAKOTA

South Dakota chose its seal 4 years before it became a state. 1889, the year of statehood, is proudly displayed in the outer ring.

South Dakota shows historic scenes of farming and industry in its seal. Natural resources and the state's natural beauty are represented with a river and rolling hills.

The Tennessee General Assembly designed a standard seal in 1987. The design shows a plow, a sheaf of wheat, and a cotton plant above the word "Agriculture." Above the word "Commerce" is a large ship representing trade.

The Roman numerals XVI, or 16, represent Tennessee as the 16th state. The year 1796 at the bottom of the seal is the year of statehood.

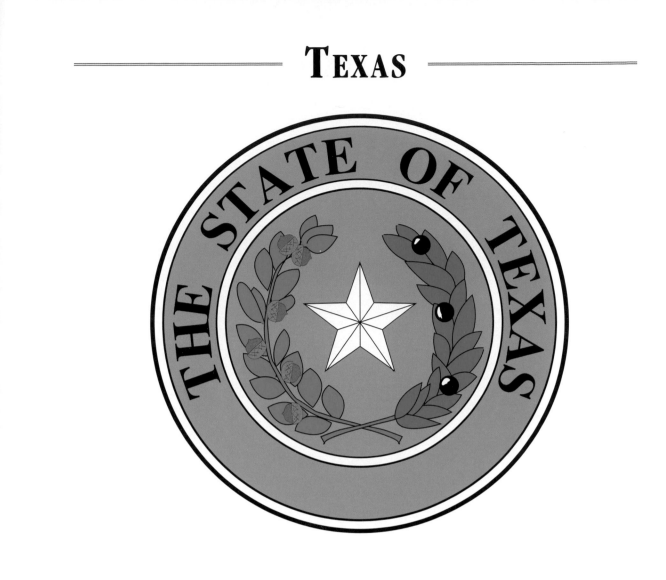

Many seals have been used for Texas. This is because of Texas history. Private governor seals, Mexican seals, and Spanish seals have all been used at one time or another. The five-pointed star is the central design of the seal today. In 1992 the Secretary of State approved this seal. The oak and olive branches around the star came from the Mexican seal design.

The early settlers of Utah used a beehive as a symbol of the region. The beehive symbol is still used today. It stands for strength in industry and strength through hard times. Utah is also nicknamed the Beehive State.

"Industry," written above the beehive, is the state motto. The year 1847, below the beehive, is the year the first pioneers entered the Great Salt Lake Valley. 1896 is the year Utah became the 45th state.

"Freedom and Unity" is the Vermont state motto. Vermont's official seal proudly displays those words. The current seal is a copy of the original one designed in 1778. After 1778 the seal changed many times. Some people felt the original design was not fancy enough. However, in 1937, the state decided the original design best represented the state.

The design of the Virginia seal was approved in 1776, two years before Virginia became the 10th state. The only words on the official seal are "Virginia," and the state motto. The motto printed at the bottom means "Thus Always to Tyrants." The images are of a Roman goddess and a tyrant, or harsh ruler. The goddess stands over the tyrant in victory. The tyrant lies helpless without his crown.

WASHINGTON

George Washington appears on the Washington state seal. A jeweler was supposed to have designed a seal with the port of Tacoma, Mt. Rainier, fields, and livestock. Instead, he drew George Washington from an image he found on a postage stamp. Another image was drawn from a picture of the President on a cough medicine crate. Today the simple portrait comes from a Gilbert Stuart painting.

The West Virginia seal has not changed since 1863, the year it was designed. The center image has a boulder engraved with the date of statehood. The boulder stands for strength and stability. Farming is represented by the farmer with his axe and plow and a stalk of corn. Industry is represented by a miner with his pick axe and an anvil and sledge hammer.

Wisconsin displays many symbols on its state seal. A shield shows a plow, a pick and shovel, an anchor, and an arm and hammer. Those images stand for Wisconsin's industry.

"E Pluribus Unum," in the center, means "out of many, one." It surrounds a shield of 13 stripes that stand for the original colonies. The farmer and the sailor represent labor on land and sea.

The Wyoming state seal displays "Equal Rights." Wyoming supported equal rights for men and women long before other states.

The seal also honors the state's major industries with the words "Livestock, Grain, Mines, and Oil." 1869 is the year Wyoming became a territory. The year 1890 is when Wyoming gained statehood.